I Can Jog!

By Cameron Macintosh

It can be fun to jog.

I can jog on a big mat.

Tap, tap, tap!

I can jog in the sun.

If it is hot, I jog in a hat.

I can jog in the mud.

Tap, tap, tap!

I can jog up to the top!

Up, up, up!

I can jog in a fun run.

I get a bib.

I jog for fun.

The dog runs to me as I jog!

Tap, tap, tap!

CHECKING FOR MEANING

1. Where are two places you can jog? *(Literal)*
2. What do joggers get to wear when they go in a fun run? *(Literal)*
3. Why should you wear a hat when it is hot? *(Inferential)*

EXTENDING VOCABULARY

fun	Look at the word *fun*. Find two other words in the text that rhyme with *fun*. Do you know any other words that rhyme with *fun*?
mud	What does the word *mud* mean? What is mud made of? Which words describe the feeling of mud in your hands?
get	Listen to the sounds in the word *get*. Which letter would you change to make the word *got*?

MOVING BEYOND THE TEXT

1. Have you ever been for a jog? Where did you go? Who went with you?
2. Where are safe places to jog near where you live? Why are they safe?
3. What is the difference between running and jogging? What other words describe the way we move? E.g. skipping, hopping, jumping.
4. In which games or sports do you need to be able to jog or run? Why?

SPEED SOUNDS

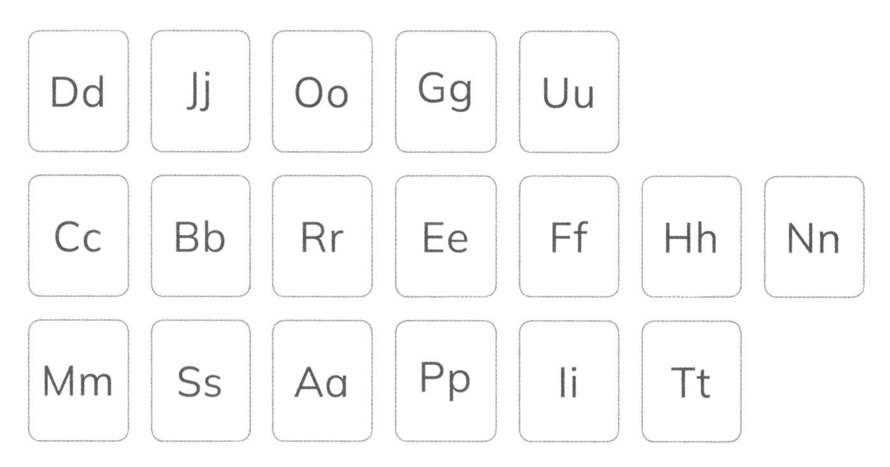

PRACTICE WORDS

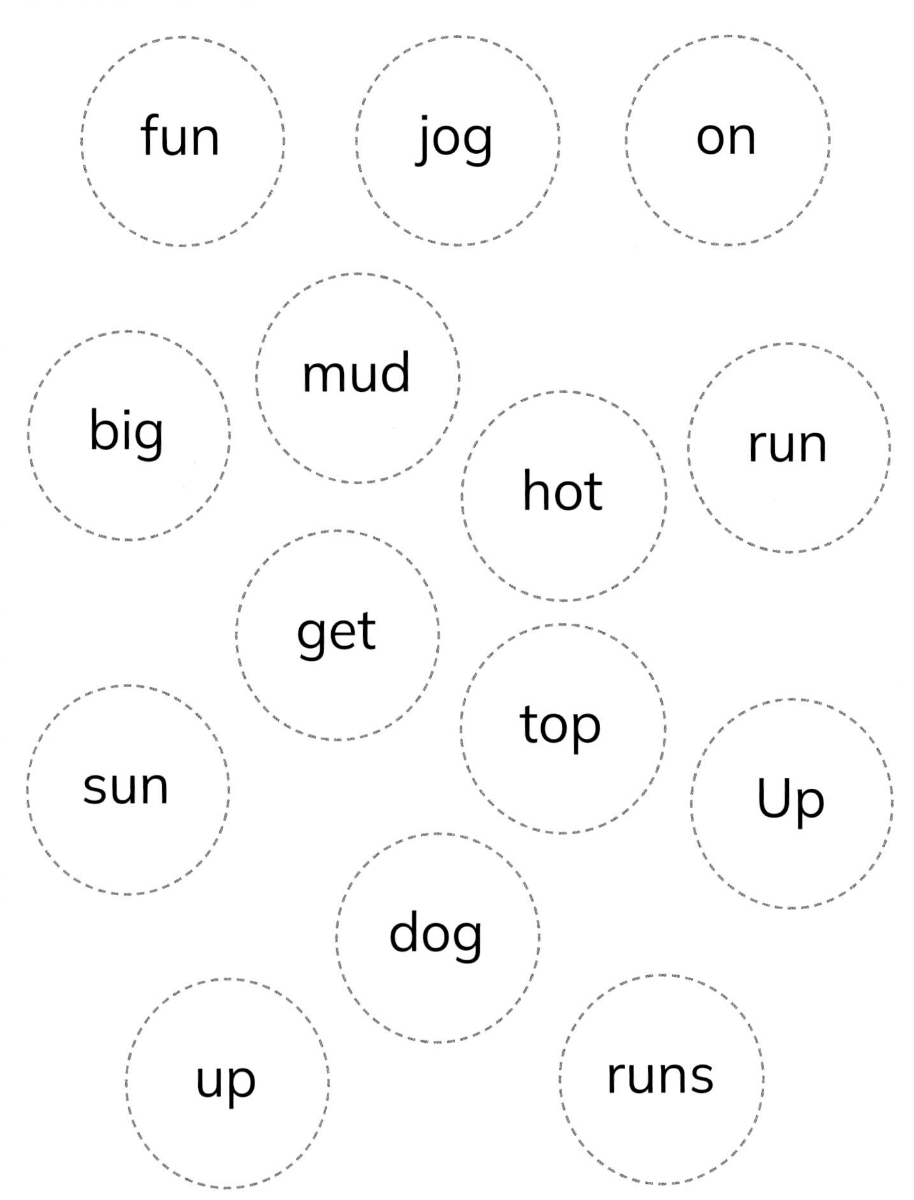